red

blue

yellow

green

purple

CD-104344

1

Read and trace each color word.

orange

brown

pink

white

black

CD-104344

Color each gumball.

Draw a line to connect each number word to the correct set.

four

five

two

three

one

zero

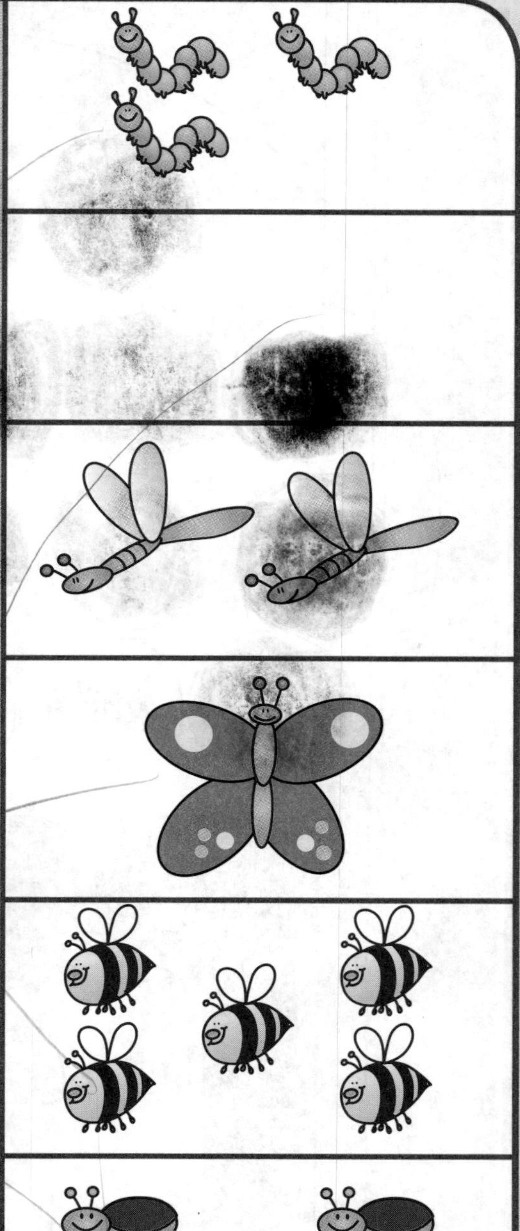

Draw a line to connect each number word to the correct set.

seven

nine

six

eight

ten

Circle the number words hidden in the puzzle. Words can be found across and down.

Word Bank

zero	one	two	three	four	five
six	seven	eight	nine	ten	

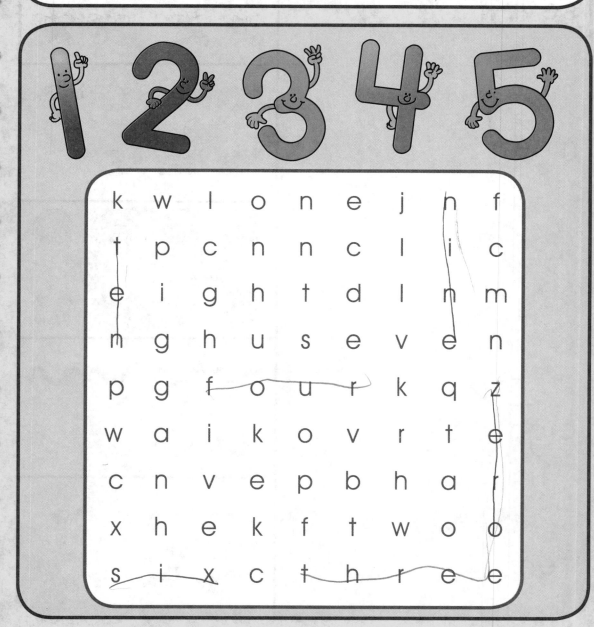

```
k w l o n e j n f
t p c n n c l i c
e i g h t d l n m
n g h u s e v e n
p g f o u r k q z
w a i k o v r t e
c n v e p b h a r
x h e k f t w o o
s i x c t h r e e
```

Read and trace each word. Color the shapes.

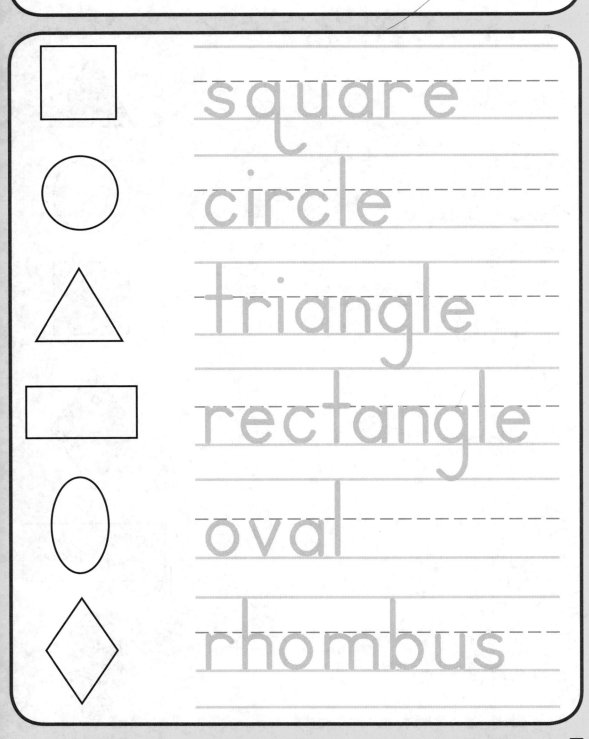

square

circle

triangle

rectangle

oval

rhombus

Draw a line to connect each word to the correct shape.

circle

rectangle

triangle

square

oval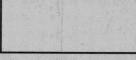

rhombus

Use the key to color the shapes.

Key

◯ = brown   ▢ = blue   ⬭ = green

△ = yellow   ▭ = purple   ◇ = black

Use the key to color the shapes.

Key

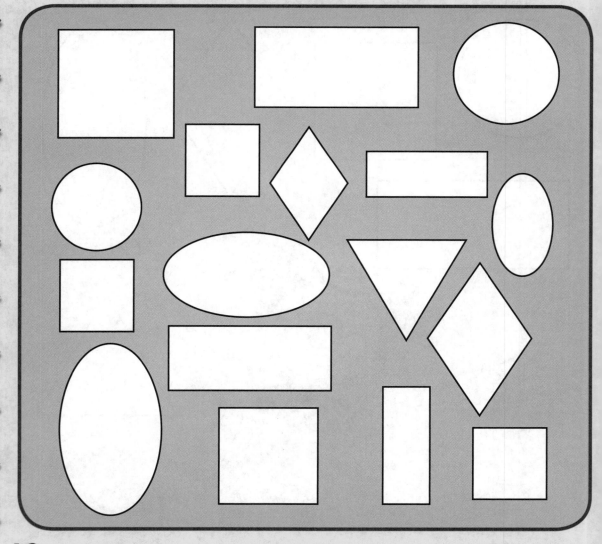

▽ = purple
◯ (oval) = orange
▭ = green

□ = red
◯ = blue
◇ = yellow

CD-104344

Read and trace each word.

pencil

paper

crayon

glue

paint

scissors

CD-104344 11

Read and trace each word.

clock

desk

chair

book

table

teacher

Circle the name of each picture.

glue   (scissors)

(desk)   chair

paint   (crayon)

pencil   (book)

(clock)   paper

(teacher)   table

CD-104344   13

Circle the words hidden in the puzzle. Words can be found across and down.

Word Bank

pencil	desk	paper	chair	glue
clock	crayon	book	scissors	teacher

```
r  e  c  r  a  y  o  n  g  o
s  i  i  h  e  b  o  o  k  t
c  c  n  g  p  a  p  e  r  e
i  c  h  a  i  r  z  y  k  a
s  r  g  u  z  t  p  h  x  c
s  i  l  f  y  m  e  l  y  h
o  r  u  t  s  w  n  c  f  e
r  d  e  s  k  o  c  g  n  r
s  o  d  u  q  b  i  r  h  y
w  f  j  f  t  c  l  o  c  k
```

CD-104344

Draw a line to connect each word to the correct picture.

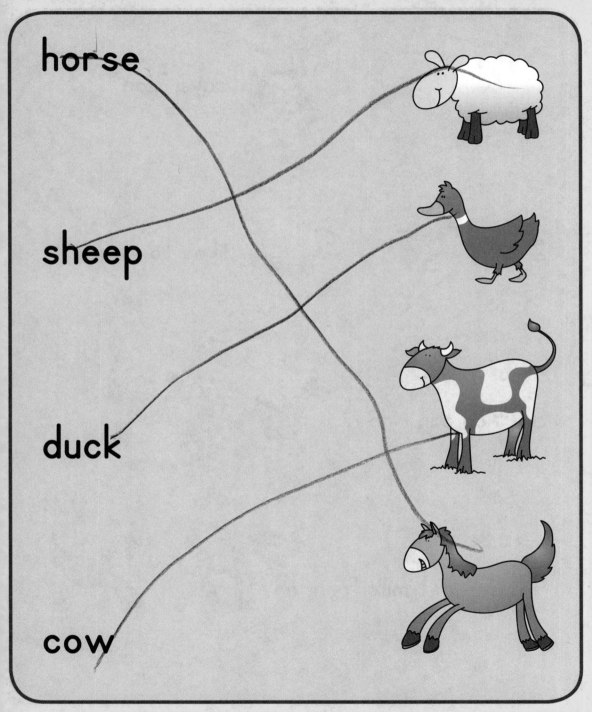

horse

sheep

duck

cow

Circle the correct animal to complete each sentence.

1. A  says, "baa."

2. A (duck) (sheep) likes to swim.

3. You can ride a (duck) (horse).

4. We get milk from a  (horse).

CD-104344

Follow the directions.

Draw a  .

Draw a around the barn.

Draw a near the barn.

Draw a behind the fence.

Draw a in the sky.

Write the missing letters to spell the word in each row three times.

1. goat ✓	g oat	g _oa_ t	goa _t_
2. barn ✓	b_a_ rn	bar_n_	b arn
3. horse ✓	_ho_rse	hor_se_	ho __ __ e
4. (farm)	far_m_	f __ rm	fa __ __
5. duck	du __ __	d __ ck	__ __ ck
6. sheep	sh __ __ p	__ __ eep	__ h __ ep
7. goose	g __ __ se	__ __ os __	goo __ __

Read and trace each word.

car

train

bus

truck

boat

airplane

Draw a line to connect each word to the correct picture.

train

car

boat

truck

bus

airplane

CD-104344

© Carson-Dellosa

Write each word from the word bank under the correct picture.

Word Bank

train　　bus　　jet　　car　　boat　　truck

Trace the paths to connect the opposites.

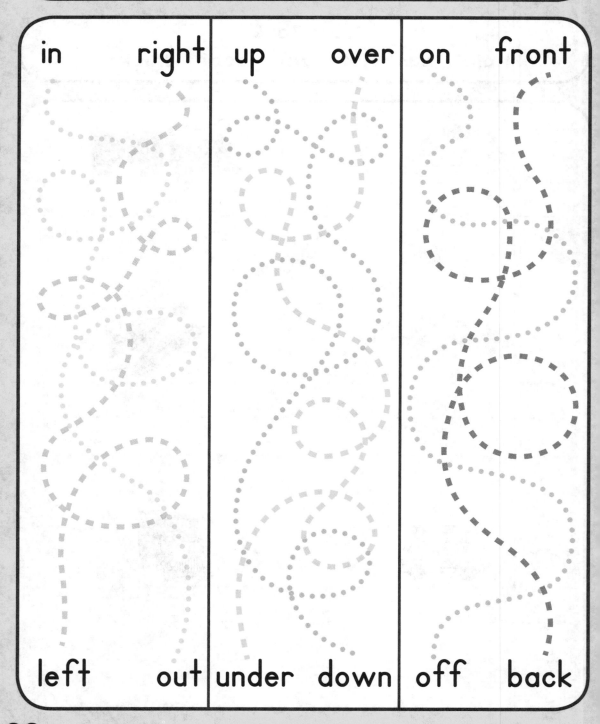

in   right   up   over   on   front

left   out   under   down   off   back

Circle the words hidden in the puzzle. Words can be found across and down.

```
a e t r d y b i g o
c i i h e f w n o b
r w o v e r e e k b
o t k s h u n d e r
s i d e t w s h x h
s m r b h e d b y d
c z o u t w d o w n
e u u t d i j g c t
f v d u p b c r h y
f f q w t y z q s t
```

Read and trace each word.

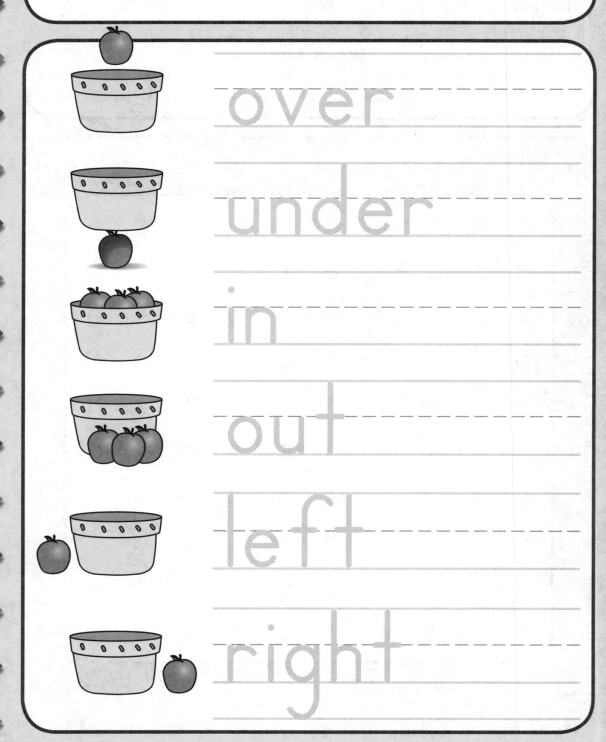

over

under

in

out

left

right

  CD-104344

Draw an X on the object in each row that does not belong.

pear	banana	fork
carrot	peas	cup
spoon	apple	blueberries
broccoli	napkin	celery
knife	orange	cherries

   CD-104344   **25**

Circle the foods that you like to eat.

apple

bread

carrot

pizza

ice cream

cheese

corn

banana

grapes

egg

orange

cake

CD-104344

Draw a line to connect each word to the correct picture.

apple

grapes

pie

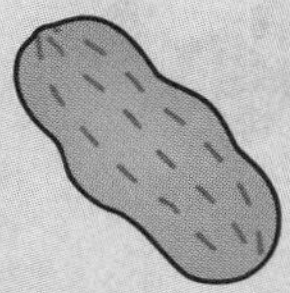

egg

peanut

pumpkin

Read and trace each word.

cat

dog

bird

fish

rabbit

hamster

CD-104344 © Carson-Dellosa

Circle the name of each picture.

hamster   dog

hen   fish

cow   rabbit

bird   horse

duck   cat

frog   sheep

Circle the animals who can be pets.

fish

dog

zebra

cat

elephant

hamster

CD-104344

Draw a line to connect each word to the correct picture.

sun

rain

snow

storm

wind

Circle the items that people wear in warm weather.

sandals

cap

jeans

T-shirt

coat

gloves

scarf

shorts

sweater

CD-104344

Circle the items that people wear in cold weather.

gloves

hat

scarf

boots

T-shirt

shorts

pants

coat

swimsuit

CD-104344

33

Draw a line from each word to the correct part of the girl.

hair

eye

nose

ear

mouth

CD-104344 © Carson-Dellosa

Draw a line from each word to the correct part of the boy.

head

arm

hand

leg

foot

Read and trace each word.

mother

father

sister

brother

baby

family

CD-104344

Write the words to make a code. Use the code to answer the question.

1. mother

2. baby

3. sister

4. uncle

5. father

What group do all of these people belong to?

A5	B2	A1	B3	D4	D2

Draw lines to connect the opposites.

big

full

happy

little

empty

sad

Draw lines to connect the opposites.

wet

under

over

cold

hot

dry

CD-104344

Circle the word that describes each picture.

hot   cold

happy   sad

little   big

dry   wet

full   empty

over   under

CD-104344

Draw lines to connect the sentences that are opposites.

The cake is big.

The boy is sad.

The ball is up.

The cake is little.

The boy is happy.

The ball is down.

 CD-104344

Circle the words hidden in the puzzle. Words can be found across and down.

Word Bank

jump   skip   run   dance   hop

s	s	j	k	u	v	m	e
u	k	w	j	i	y	r	h
r	i	q	b	r	u	n	d
p	p	r	a	p	i	j	a
a	d	a	n	c	e	u	z
b	g	h	h	v	u	m	s
v	s	v	o	h	r	p	p
z	g	u	p	i	l	w	m

CD-104344

Draw a line to connect each word to the correct picture.

spoon

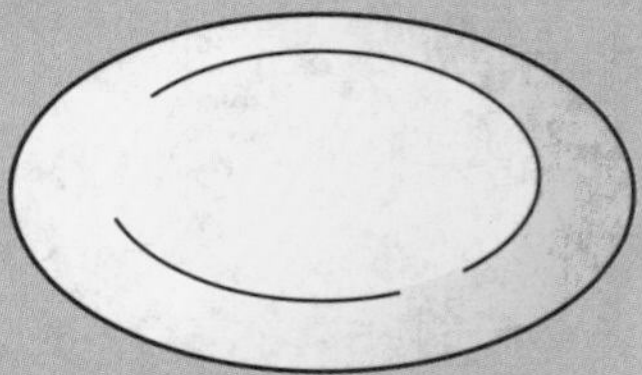

fork

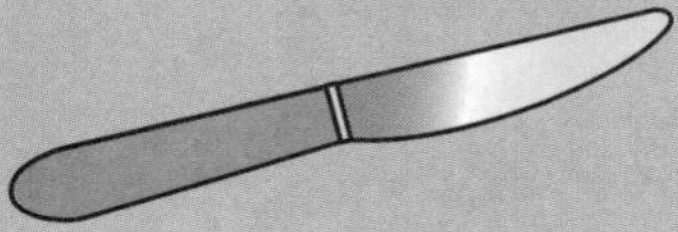

plate

bowl

cup

knife

Circle the name of each picture.

fork   spoon

plate   bowl

cup   bowl

knife   fork

knife   cup

plate   spoon

CD-104344

Circle the name of each picture.

net
pet
set

bed
red
fed

let
set
wet

jet
bet
met

let
get
net

wed
red
sled

CD-104344

Circle the name of each picture.

triangle   square

mother   father

hen   horse

clock   desk

car   airplane

hand   foot

CD-104344

Circle the words hidden in the puzzle. Words can be found across and down.

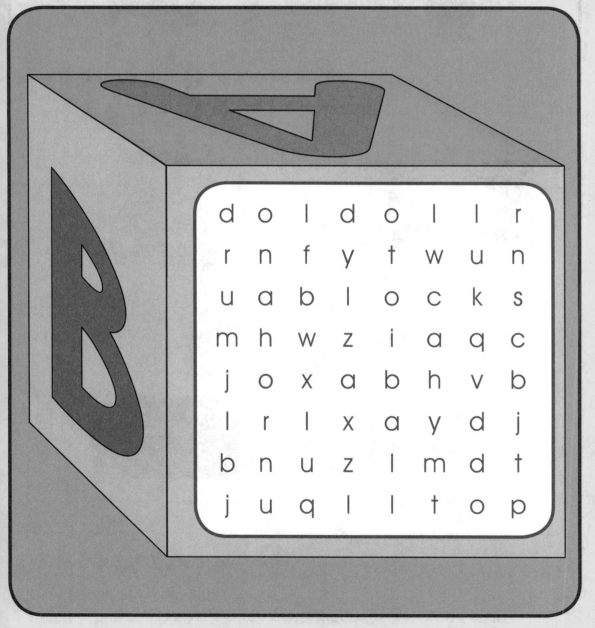

```
d o l d o l l r
r n f y t w u n
u a b l o c k s
m h w z i a q c
j o x a b h v b
l r l x a y d j
b n u z l m d t
j u q l l t o p
```

Read and trace each word.

lamp

tub

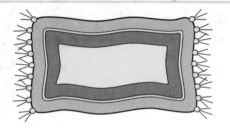

rug

bed

sink

couch

CD-104344

Circle the objects that you might see at home.

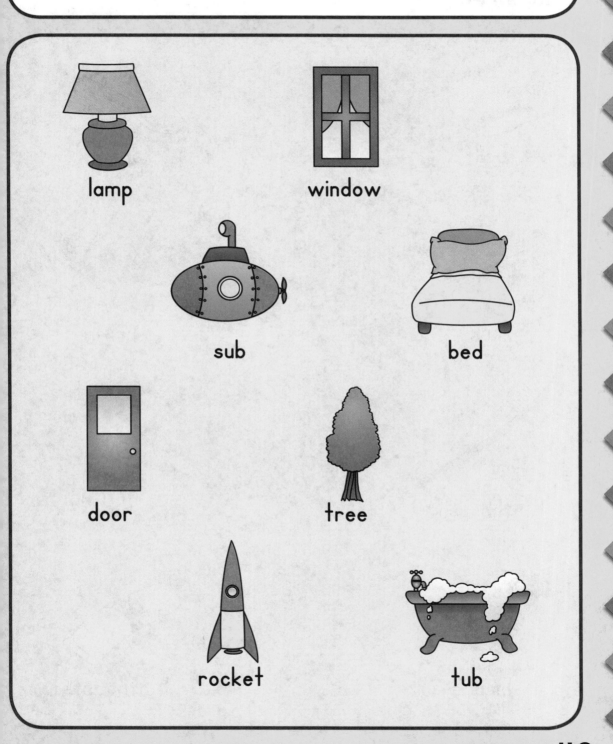

lamp

window

sub

bed

door

tree

rocket

tub

CD-104344

49

Draw lines to connect the objects that belong together.

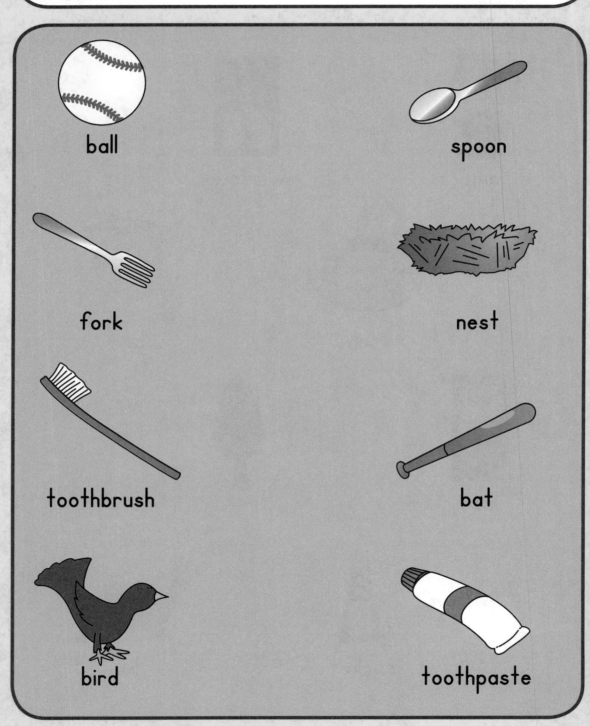

ball

spoon

fork

nest

toothbrush

bat

bird

toothpaste

Circle the object that belongs with the first object in each row.

bee	hive	car	cup
sock	sun	shoe	drum
dog	leash	clock	kite
needle	ring	boat	thread
moon	apple	stars	stamp

CD-104344 **51**

Draw lines to connect the objects that belong together. Circle the words hidden in the puzzle.

pencil

tracks

dog

chair

train

paper

table

bone

q h p b o n e z t e
e f a e c b a x r t
y a p e n c i l a t
i n e m d o c k c r
d p r e o f g m k a
k v p r g i e t s i
t x m t a b l e y n
j z g w z c h a i r

 CD-104344

Circle the picture that matches each sentence.

It is a tree.

It is a ball.

It is a bus.

It is a spoon.

CD-104344

Circle the sentence that describes each picture.

This is a cat.

This is a dog.

This is one frog.

This is two frogs.

The turtle is big.

The cow is big.

The rabbit can hop.

The girl has a book.

The truck is big.

The cat is on a chair.

Circle the sentence that describes each picture.

This is three apples.

This is five apples.

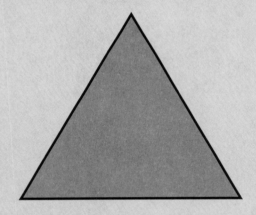

This is a square.

This is a triangle.

The paint is red.

The paint is blue.

CD-104344

Circle the picture that completes each sentence.

1. A  is green.

  frog   cow

2. A  is orange.

  carrot   banana

3.  are purple.

  Grapes Oranges

4. The  is yellow.

  bus   car

Circle the picture that completes each sentence.

1. A  has leaves.

man   tree

2. A  can play softball.

ring   girl

3. A  is big.

horse   mouse

4. A  can jump.

frog   fan

Write the name of each picture to complete each sentence.

Dan's _____ _____ _____ sat on a

big _____ _____ _____. Dan was a

nice _____ _____ _____. He had a

purple _____ _____ _____. He had a

new _____ _____ _____.

He is wearing a coat.

It is raining.

She baked a cake.

The baby is crawling.

Read and trace each sentence. Draw a picture that matches the sentence.

The car is blue.

A bird can fly.

Read and trace each sentence. Draw a picture that matches the sentence.

I like ice cream!

She has a dog.

CD-104344   © Carson-Dellosa

In each box, color the three squares with words that rhyme. The first one has been done for you.

twig	lip	wit
fin	fig	win
dip	sit	wig

pin	lick	hill
chin	mill	fit
fill	pick	pit

wig	brick	dig
him	trick	sit
hip	sick	tin

thick	sit	fill
spin	skin	twin
mist	fib	did

 CD-104344

Circle the words that rhyme.

ten	hot	hen	wig
pen	men	kit	cab
tan	den	tack	then

Say the name of each picture. Write a word that rhymes with each name.

_____

_____

_____

_____

_____

_____

_____

_____

_____

CD-104344